SLAVERY
IN AMERICA

HOW SLAVES BUILT
AMERICA

By Duchess Harris, JD, PhD
with Tom Streissguth

Essential Library

An Imprint of Abdo Publishing | abdobooks.com

ABDOBOOKS.COM

Published by Abdo Publishing, a division of ABDO, PO Box 398166, Minneapolis, Minnesota 55439. Copyright © 2020 by Abdo Consulting Group, Inc. International copyrights reserved in all countries. No part of this book may be reproduced in any form without written permission from the publisher. Essential Library™ is a trademark and logo of Abdo Publishing.

Printed in the United States of America, North Mankato, Minnesota.
022019
092019

THIS BOOK CONTAINS
RECYCLED MATERIALS

Cover Photo: Kean Collection/Archive Photos/Getty Images
Interior Photos: Everett Historical/Shutterstock Images, 4–5, 19, 34–35, 44, 66–67, 73; Bob Pool/Shutterstock Images, 9; North Wind Picture Archives, 12–13, 29, 69; iStockphoto, 22, 32, 46–47, 48, 52, 63, 77; MPI/Archive Photos/Getty Images, 24–25; Smith Collection/Gado/Archive Photos/Getty Images, 39; The Print Collector/Alamy, 56–57; Picture History/Newscom, 59; Walter Oleksy/Alamy, 64; Lightfoot/Archive Photos/Getty Images, 78–79; Buyenlarge/Archive Photos/Getty Images, 81; Red Line Editorial, 83; Oklahoma Historical Society/Archive Photos/Getty Images, 86–87, 90; David Goldman/AP Images, 93

Editor: Alyssa Krekelberg
Series Designer: Laura Graphenteen

LIBRARY OF CONGRESS CONTROL NUMBER: 2018965962

PUBLISHER'S CATALOGING-IN-PUBLICATION DATA

Names: Harris, Duchess, author | Streissguth, Tom, author.
Title: How slaves built America / by Duchess Harris and Tom Streissguth
Description: Minneapolis, Minnesota: Abdo Publishing, 2020 | Series: Slavery in America | Includes online resources and index.
Identifiers: ISBN 9781532119248 (lib. bdg.) | ISBN 9781532173424 (ebook)
Subjects: LCSH: Slavery--United States--History--Juvenile literature. | Slavery--Southern States--History--Juvenile literature. | Slavery--United States--Colonization--Juvenile literature. | Enslaved persons--Juvenile literature.
Classification: DDC 326.9--dc23

CONTENTS

CHAPTER ONE

WHAT SLAVERY BUILT

I n the summer of 1792, the sound of iron handpicks chiseling sandstone could be heard for some distance from Aquia Creek, Virginia. On a place now known as Government Island, crews of men toiled long days, digging and cutting the rock. Oxcarts brought the cut stone to a ship landing, where it was put aboard deep-bottomed ships for transport.

The toiling stonecutters were not the first on this small island, which covered just 17 acres (6.9 ha). For a century, Aquia stone had been cut and shaped into walls, foundations, steps, fireplaces, and grave markers. Now the rock was going about 40 miles (64 km) up the nearby Potomac River to a stretch of empty, low-lying

Enslaved people helped build Washington, DC.

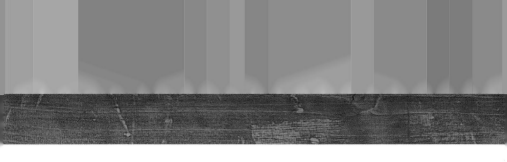

ground, where settlers had long avoided the muddy, mosquito-infested swamps.[1]

An architect named Pierre L'Enfant owned the island. L'Enfant needed the stone, not the land. He had work to do as the appointed architect of a new city on the banks of the Potomac. And to build that city, he would need stonecutters, masons, sawyers, brickmakers, carpenters, and drivers.

FOUNDING OF A CAPITAL CITY

In 1790, Congress had designated land along the Potomac's eastern bank as the location of a new capital. At this spot, there would be buildings for the legislature, federal departments, and the president's home. This area would be called the District of Columbia—later known as Washington, DC—and would not belong to any state. It lay between Maryland and Virginia—two of the original British colonies that still allowed slavery.

In their search for laborers to build the new city, the commissioners of the District of Columbia at first wanted to use indentured servants and

BENJAMIN BANNEKER

When Pierre L'Enfant suddenly quit as the architect building Washington, DC, Benjamin Banneker was asked to join the planning committee. Banneker, who had both white and black ancestry, was free. He helped map out the Washington, DC, parks, streets, and buildings.

workers brought from Europe. However, they couldn't find enough laborers this way. To meet the demand, the architects of the city rented enslaved people from slaveholders who lived nearby. James Hoban, the architect of the White House, brought four of his own slaves to the work. His assistant, Pierce Purcell, brought one as well.

To build the president's house, slaves cleared the land of trees and brush. They dug foundations and hauled the bricks and stone into place. According to official White House records, dozens of slave laborers worked at the site. The records list them by first name only: Peter, Ben, Harry, Newton, and Moses, among many others. Next to each slave's name is the amount due to his owner: as much as $60 a year.[2]

It took about eight years for the laborers—slave, free, and indentured—to complete the White House. In 1800, John Adams

THE GOING RATE

Architect James Hoban earned $60 for the labor of each of the four slaves he sent to work on the White House. Today, people who support paying reparations for slavery believe that the descendants of these laborers should, finally, be compensated for their work. By the calculation of author Michael Daly, to Hoban's $60 we should add 5 percent interest, compounded annually since 1792, and then translate the result into the value of money in 2016. The resulting debt comes to more than $3 million. For all the work done by slaves on the presidential home, Daly calculates the total bill in modern times is $83 million.[3]

became the first president to live there. A Founding Father from the state of Massachusetts, Adams was an opponent of slavery and owned no slaves. But several future presidents, including Thomas Jefferson, James Madison, Andrew Jackson, and John Tyler, did rely on slaves to run their households and work as servants.

In 2016, First Lady Michelle Obama reminded people of the White House's history. "I wake up every morning in a house that was built by slaves," she said.[4] The White House isn't the only structure in Washington, DC, with this history. Enslaved workers also helped build the Capitol Building and many of the homes, commercial buildings, and churches in the city. In addition, slaves worked on the farms that supplied the area with food, tobacco, and the raw material for clothing.

Washington, DC, was not the only city in the United States partially built with slave labor, nor

Restrictions on the White House

Although slaves worked in the White House before the Civil War (1861–1865), they were not permitted as guests or visitors. This prohibition continued after the war, when segregation of the races prevailed throughout the country. There was one exception: the annual Easter egg hunt on the South Lawn of the White House. On one day of the year, white and black guests mingled as children chased down painted eggs, which was an Easter tradition.

Today, people can tour Mount Vernon and learn about the enslaved people who lived there.

was it the first. In the late 1600s, slaves helped raise the Castillo de San Marcos, the oldest surviving fort in the country, in Saint Augustine, Florida. The architects of New York City's famous Trinity Church also rented slaves to build the structure. Slaves helped build the University of Virginia, founded by President Jefferson. They worked on Jefferson's plantation at Monticello, Virginia. And they helped raise Mount Vernon, the home of George Washington.

Fighting for the Country

Black soldiers have been fighting for the United States since well before the Civil War and the end of slavery that followed. Enslaved people served in the Continental Army and Navy during the Revolutionary War. Some of them also joined forces with the British.

Jordan Noble, a freed slave from Georgia, joined the US army during the War of 1812 (1812–1815). Noble was not the only black person in the forces fighting in 1814. There were about 900 black people who volunteered to fight as General Andrew Jackson gathered his defenses to fend off a British attack on New Orleans, Louisiana.[5]

Noble was a drummer whose main task was to keep a steady drumbeat going to keep soldiers in rank and marching together. Using prearranged signals, he conveyed important orders to the US troops and helped bring about the defeat of the British at the Battle of New Orleans. This victory won the southern reaches of the Mississippi River for the United States. Noble stayed in the military through the Civil War before retiring in New Orleans as a widely recognized military hero.

The Contribution

The US economy was founded with large contributions from people who were enslaved. Legally, these people could be bought, sold, transported, and forced to labor for a lifetime. The issue of slavery divided the nation and eventually brought about the Civil War (1861–1865), in which the proslavery group of states split from the rest of the nation, called the Union. Some freed slaves served on the Union side in that conflict. In fact, African Americans had been enlisting in the country's armed forces since the Revolutionary War (1775–1783).

Following the Civil War and the end of slavery, the South went through Reconstruction, when former slaves fought to claim their place as free and equal citizens. Jim Crow laws continued to separate the races for decades. The struggle of African Americans to overcome discrimination remains a key issue for the United States today. The country's modern political debates and divisions can trace their roots, in large part, to slavery, the Civil War, and Reconstruction.

Slavery played a big role in the founding and growth of banks, insurance companies, railroads, and industries such as textile production. And individuals who were enslaved contributed to major inventions, such as the McCormick reaper, a harvesting device. The effects of slavery echo into today's society, and there's no question that enslaved people helped build America.

DISCUSSION STARTERS

- Do you think it's important to remember the contributions African Americans have made to the United States? Explain your answer.

- Why would the use of enslaved people to build the White House still cause controversy today?

- What do you think fighting for the Union cause during the Civil War meant for free and enslaved African Americans?

CHAPTER TWO

CHARLESTON

The ship drifted in from the sea and dropped anchor. After departing from Bermuda, an island in the Atlantic Ocean, the ship had lost sight of two companion ships in a heavy storm. Soon after, it arrived at the flat and dreary coast of what would eventually be South Carolina. It was the spring of 1670, and aboard the ship were settlers, indentured servants, and slaves.

The British colony of Charles Town, which would later be named Charleston, thrived after its founding by the crew and passengers of the ship. The surrounding land was cleared by slaves. The slaveholders ordered the people they enslaved to grow sugarcane. It was brutally hard work made worse by the heat and the threat of disease. Malaria, spread by the abundant mosquitoes, killed most slaves within a few years. Life was dangerous for

Ports were important to growing colonial cities because they were essential to trade.

the town-dwelling settlers as well. Pirates raided along
the coast. Several Native American tribes, including the
Yamasee, sought to repel the people who had invaded
their land.

IN THE LOW COUNTRY

Named for King Charles II, Charles Town was the first
settlement in the Low Country of South Carolina. The
Low Country included the coastal regions of South
Carolina and Georgia. Like other colonies, such as Virginia
and Maryland, South Carolina allowed slavery, but most
Low Country slaves came from the Caribbean sugar
islands, including Jamaica and Barbados. They were one or
two generations removed from parents and grandparents
who were kidnapped on the west coast of Africa and sent
across the ocean to work.

In South Carolina, slaves cleared the land, cut wood for
homes, barns, and fences, and planted the first crops. They
were a key factor in the settlement of the colony. Without
slaves, sugar cultivation was impossible. Paid laborers
would have been too expensive to use, if any could even
have been found. The more slaves, the larger a sugar
plantation could grow, and the more profitable it was for
the white men who owned it.

As slaves who arrived with the original settlers died
from disease, harsh working conditions, old age, or other

causes, Low Country landowners began importing captives from Africa. Demand was strong—the vast acreages inland needed more and more slaves. English investors established the Royal African Company to carry out slave trading between the west coast of Africa and the North American colonies.

Planters in South Carolina paid on average 100 to 200 pounds for a slave. In modern money converted to US dollars, that is between $11,630 and $23,200.[1] The slaves worked in bad conditions in coastal rice fields. The work was hard, dirty, and dangerous. Malaria, yellow fever, and other illnesses were common.

KEEPING THE CULTURE

Diseases such as malaria and yellow fever were rampant in the Low Country. Fearing illness, white slaveholders spent much of their time away from their land. This allowed an isolated, largely African population to maintain their language and traditions in the coastal regions and islands of South Carolina.

Slaves enjoying minimal independence from white control and interference managed to build their own communities. After the Civil War and emancipation, the Gullah people survived on the Sea Islands, which line the Atlantic coasts of South Carolina and Georgia. The Gullah have kept many African cultural traditions into the present day. They tell African folktales, use African names, and speak a language similar to a dialect used in the West African nation of Sierra Leone.

The high demand for slavery, and the good profits in the slave-importing business, made Charleston the busiest slave market in the British colonies. During the colonial period, about 40 percent of all slaves brought to North America passed through Charleston.[2]

A New Cash Crop

As they moved and settled inland, Low Country landowners turned to a new cash crop: rice. This crop grew in low-lying, well-watered coastal areas. But new varieties of rice also made cultivation possible away from the coastal lowlands. Using brokers in Charleston, rice growers sold their product to English merchant brokers, who resold it to traders, who then shipped it to Europe, the Mediterranean region, and India. Worldwide demand for rice was high, and the trade was profitable. By the order of their king, English brokers gained the exclusive right to buy it from the English colonies.

The rice trade built Charleston into one of the wealthiest cities in colonial America. South Carolina exported around 10,000 pounds (4,500 kg) of rice in 1698, 131,000 pounds (59,400 kg) in 1699, and 394,000 pounds (179,000 kg) in 1700.[3] By 1726, Charleston was exporting millions of pounds of rice each year. The city's seaport also bustled from the trade in indigo and cotton.

A City Apologizes

On June 20, 2018, the city of Charleston issued a formal apology for its role in the slave-built economy. The apology came at the end of a debate over the issue in a Charleston City Council meeting. Not everyone in the city agreed that an apology was necessary. People asked, why apologize when slavery ended so long ago and nobody alive still owns slaves or takes part in the slave trade?

In some ways, Charleston still whitewashes its history, as historians Ethan Kytle and Blain Roberts explain in their book *Denmark Vesey's Garden*. In the past, slaves were known as servants in Charleston. Slave traders called themselves auctioneers or brokers, and homes built for slaves were called carriage houses. "We really see [the debate over an apology] as a battle of two memory traditions," remarked the historians—and in fact, the result was close.[4] Meeting in the slave-built Charleston City Hall, the council voted seven to five to officially condemn the slave trade.

In the middle of the 1700s, Charleston was the busiest port in the North American colonies.

Rice attracted new settlers to South Carolina. However, relying on a single crop posed problems. The price of rice rose and fell with the supply, which varied from one year to the next. When growers brought in a big harvest, the price fell, bringing hard times. Reducing the supply would support the price, but unlike other colonies, South Carolina took no action to limit production.

Rice growers needed slaves, and in large numbers. The costs to growers for their labor, equipment, and land were high. As a result, only those growers with easy access to loans, credit, and money persevered. They bought small plots and combined them into large estates. In this way began the Southern plantation system, in which wealthy landowners grew cash crops using large communities of slaves.

In his article "The Colonial Rice Trade," historian Henry C. Dethloff explains: "Fortunes could be made and lost in a season. Market conditions, milling costs, and cultivation practices contributed to the concentration of landholdings and large-scale, mass production and marketing techniques, and to the expansion of the slave system."[5]

Technology and Slavery

Growers used a system of dams, canals, and artificial ponds for flooding rice fields by 1720. This reserve system, built by slaves on the rice plantations, allowed growers to collect and distribute water to planted fields. This made the rice crop less dependent on rain.

In 1750, a new system came into use. Ocean tides forced fresh water back up coastal rivers, raising the water level and forcing floodgates open. When the tide went out, the gates closed, thus preserving a reservoir and a continuous supply of fresh water for use. The system made

Southern rice production eventually started to decline after the Civil War.

water supply to rice more reliable and enlarged the area where the crop could be cultivated.

Rice farmers no longer had to depend on rainfall for the success of their harvest, but they needed slaves to build the levees and dams required for the watering system. By the first decade of the 1700s, African slaves outnumbered white residents in South Carolina. A total of 131 slaves were brought to the area in 1710, and between 1,000 and 2,000 slaves arrived each year from 1720 to 1776.[6] At a time when northeastern states were banning slavery, the Low Country and Charleston were thriving on slave labor.

ENRICHING THE LOW COUNTRY

In the 1700s, rice cultivation spread along the Carolina coast and south to Georgia, where the towns of Savannah, Beaufort, and Georgetown all thrived. Some of the wealthiest men in the North American colonies, including future South Carolina governor Thomas Pinckney, grew rich on the rice trade, which also supported Charleston's brokers, traders, agents, shippers, and millers.

The import and export firm of Henry Laurens of Charleston thrived by charging commissions to rice planters to handle their trade with England. Laurens and other merchants also provided credit to planters, who had to borrow money

SLAVE CODES

Slavery built a major part of South Carolina's law as well as its economy. Slave codes that set out restrictions on slaves as well as their holders were abundant and constantly changing. At one point, a slaveholder needed an act of the state legislature to free a slave. White people had the authority to arrest and punish slaves for any violation of the law. Slaves could not wear certain fabrics considered above their social position. They could not write, own weapons, or play horns or drums.

The motivation behind these laws was the fear of a slave revolt. The laws survived in a different form after the Civil War, as South Carolina and other formerly slaveholding states passed Black Codes that were meant to keep freed African Americans separate from and unequal to whites.

CHARLESTON HISTORY

Once a busy seaport, Charleston now attracts visitors with beautiful old homes and commercial buildings, some dating to the 1700s. There's an important, darker part of Charleston history that's on display as well. One of the major stops on tours of the city is the Old Slave Mart at 6 Chalmers Street. This museum was once a place where slaves were sold at auctions.

The museum was first established by Miriam Wilson, a native of Ohio whose father fought for the Union side in the Civil War. Wilson collected artifacts and documents relating to the local slave trade and opened the Old Slave Mart to the public in 1938.

Not everyone in Charleston was happy about the city's new tourist attraction. Some accused Wilson of digging up bad memories and a tragic side of its history for her own profit. To this day, some people see her as cleaning up history for the enjoyment of tourists.

to purchase tools, slaves, seeds, and other supplies. They also contracted with New England shippers to transport the rice to England and, when permitted, directly to European ports. While the rice trade thrived alongside the trade in African slaves, the profits from slavery built great fortunes and stately homes in Newport, Rhode Island; Boston, Massachusetts; New York City; and Charleston.

This slavery-based system was the backbone of the colonial economy. Using rice as collateral, bankers throughout the colonies extended credit to growers and middlemen, building the early foundation of a national banking and credit system. Rice also supported colonial

In the 1800s, Charleston was a prospering city.

governments with taxes, fees, and tolls charged for the
crop's shipment.

A Wealthy City

This thriving trade built Charleston into one of the
wealthiest cities in the colonies. The town was built on a
modern grid pattern, in contrast to the chaotic medieval
street plans of cities in Europe. Elegant homes, churches,
and public buildings delighted visitors in the 1700s, as they
still do today.

   Writing in 1709, a visitor named John Lawson
described the scene:

> *The Town has very regular and fair Streets, in which*
> *are good Buildings of Brick and Wood, and since my*

coming thence, has had great Additions of beautiful,

large Brick-buildings, besides a strong Fort, and regular

Fortifications made to defend the Town. The Inhabitants,

by their wise Management and Industry, have much

improv'd the Country [colony], which is in as thriving

Circumstances at this Time as any Colony on the

Continent of English America.[7]

In his account, Lawson went into great detail on the business of the city, describing the work of merchants, growers, and shippers. However, he took no interest in the contribution of forced labor to Charleston's prosperity and fine appearance. The subject of slavery and the slave trade didn't interest him; instead, he simply passed it by. But this area and the rest of the United States owe a great deal to the forced work of enslaved people.

DISCUSSION STARTERS

- Have you learned about the contributions of enslaved people in any of your school history classes? If so, what did you learn? If not, why do you think the topic wasn't taught?

- Do you think cities such as Charleston should apologize for allowing slavery in the past? Explain your answer.

- What do you think people should do if they find out a company is selling products that were produced with slave labor?

CHAPTER THREE

COMPROMISES WITH SLAVERY

On a freezing cold, rainy December day in the year 1799, former president George Washington set out on horseback from his home in Mount Vernon, Virginia. After returning home, he fell ill. Tremors racked his feverish body, and his throat began closing up. Slowly but surely, he was suffocating. The doctors could do nothing but uselessly draw blood. Washington knew the end was near. But before his last hours passed, there was something he had to do.

Washington called for two documents to be brought from his writing desk. Examining both, he gave instructions to his wife. He told her one of the documents was to be burned. In the other,

At one point, George Washington had hundreds of enslaved people at Mount Vernon.

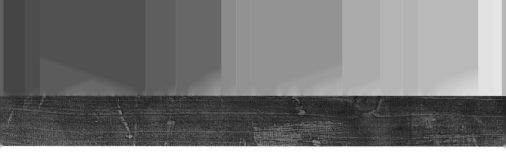

he had found the words he sought: "Upon the decease [of] my wife, it is my Will & desire th[at] all the Slaves which I hold in [my] *own right*, shall receive their free[dom]."[1] Washington laid his last will and testament aside. He died the next day and was buried on the prosperous estate he had built and maintained with the use of slave labor.

CASH CROP: TOBACCO

Washington owned his first slaves at the age of 11. Many years later, through his marriage to Martha Custis in 1759, he gained 17,000 acres (6,900 ha) and more than 200 slaves who belonged to his new wife.[2] This was abundant labor and land to grow the colony's leading cash crop, tobacco. But Washington fell into debt, a common problem for planters who needed lots of money to run big farming operations.

Tobacco made the fortunes of several prominent Virginia planters. In the 1720s, tobacco leaves were used as a form of money, and in many places, they could be used instead

ONEY JUDGE: WASHINGTON'S SLAVE

Oney Judge was one of Washington's slaves. She fled the White House in 1796 after learning that she was to be given to Martha's granddaughter as a gift. Judge successfully made it to New Hampshire, but Washington made attempts to find her. He discovered where she was and demanded that she be apprehended. Judge was never captured, but she was a fugitive for the rest of her life.

of scarce coins. There was high demand in Europe and throughout the colonies for Virginia tobacco, but it was a labor-intensive crop. Tobacco seeds had to be planted and then transplanted. Laborers had to weed the ground and cut the plants to encourage leaf growth. After harvest, they set out the leaves for drying.

Tobacco couldn't be grown profitably without slaves. For that reason, the Virginia Assembly passed laws meant to strengthen slavery. One law in 1705 said, "all servants imported and brought into this country, by sea or land, who were not Christians in their native country . . . shall be slaves, and as such be here bought and sold notwithstanding a conversion to Christianity afterwards."[3]

Many leaders of the Revolutionary War were slave-owning planters. By the 1770s, they had a long list of

TOBACCO AND THE REVOLUTION

On the outbreak of the Revolutionary War, the colonies found they needed money, and a lot of it, to pay for their war against the British. To finance independence, Benjamin Franklin arranged a loan from France. To secure the loan, he pledged millions of pounds of Virginia tobacco, grown and harvested with slave labor. This helpful loan was still not enough—the Continental Army was consistently short of funds to pay its soldiers. Appealing for help to his fellow colonists, the army's leader, General George Washington, declared, "If you can't send money, send tobacco."[4]

grievances against the British who governed them. One of the most important for Virginians was the tobacco tax. This charge was paid through British merchants who handled tobacco exported from the colonies. The tax contributed to the heavy debts that were driving many tobacco farmers out of business.

INDEPENDENCE

Washington, Jefferson, Madison, and other colonial landowners drafted a list of grievances against the British into a case for independence. In the Declaration of Independence, signed in 1776, the colonists asserted their natural right to "Life, Liberty and the pursuit of Happiness."[5] They claimed the right to establish their own government in which elected representatives, instead of the British parliament, made the laws.

Freedom from heavy British taxes would also benefit them, while the end of British governance on trade would help landowners and merchants throughout the colonies. However, the independence they eventually won brought about a ban on their tobacco exports by the British government. This cost Virginia and Maryland their principal European tobacco markets.

By 1787, the year the Constitution was ratified, the future of slavery in the United States was in jeopardy. Several Northern states took steps to abolish slavery,

The majority of US Founding Fathers were slaveholders.

and Virginia had passed a law years earlier banning the importation of slaves. There were also economic forces working against slavery. Caribbean plantations that grew cash crops were competing with the United States and reducing US exports of slave-grown commodities such as rice and tobacco.

But Southern landowners fought to preserve slavery— they believed their plantations and livelihoods depended on it. Independence had been won from the British, and the former colonies had priorities of their own. New York, for example, thrived from foreign trade, immigration from Europe, and a growing manufacturing sector, while South Carolina was dependent on the export of rice and indigo. There was a strong movement to abolish slavery in the New England states, and Northern abolitionists were seen as a threat in Southern states such as Georgia. The divisions

in the young nation—mainly between the Northern
and Southern states—threatened to break the United
States apart.

Defining a Person

By 1787, US leaders realized they needed a framework
of laws and principles that would apply to all the states
and hold the country together. They met in Philadelphia,
Pennsylvania, to debate thorny issues, including slavery,
and hammer out details. The result was a document
that began with one of the most famous sentences in US
history: "We the people of the United States, in order to
form a more perfect union . . . do ordain and establish this
Constitution for the United States of America."[6]

At this Constitutional Convention, Northern
and Southern representatives made some important
compromises. The importation of slaves—essential for
Southern agriculture and a key to profitable business for
Northern shipping interests—was protected from any
ban until 1808. In addition, the fugitive slave clause in the
Constitution required runaway slaves to be returned to
their owners, no matter where they were caught. Also,
Southern representatives agreed to allow the federal
government to require goods to be shipped on US vessels.
Previously, Southern traders had used British merchant
ships for transport. The exclusive right granted by federal

A Slaveholder against Slavery

George Mason was a wealthy Virginia landowner. Unlike many plantation owners of the 1700s, he did not want the United States to remain a slaveholding nation. "Every master of slaves is born a petty tyrant," wrote Mason—although he was the second-largest slaveholder, after George Washington, in Virginia's Fairfax County.[7]

Sent by Virginia to the Constitutional Convention of 1787, Mason found himself at odds with the other delegates over several points. For example, he opposed the admission of Southern states into the union until they abolished slavery. Unable to persuade the other delegates with their arguments, Mason and two other men refused to sign the Constitution. However, Mason remained a slaveholder for the rest of his life.

law was a great benefit to Northern shipowners and to the bustling ports that relied on overseas trade, such as Boston, New York City, and Newport.

As for slaves under the Constitution, were they property or were they people? Representation in Congress depended on population: the more people in a state, the more members it sent to the House of Representatives. If counted as people for the purposes of representation, slaves would give the Southern states an advantage in the legislature. If they weren't counted, then the Northern states—where most of the country's free citizens lived—would hold much greater power in Congress.

Frederick Douglass broke barriers for African Americans. For example, in the mid-1800s he was nominated as a presidential candidate.

Slavery also affected the issue of federal taxes, which were based on the amount of property an individual owned. If counted as property for taxation, slaves would cost the Southern states more in payments to the federal government. If slaves didn't count for taxes, then the Northern states would have a much heavier tax burden.

So the framers of the Constitution came up with the three-fifths compromise. In the census that counted residents every ten years, a slave would count as three-fifths of a person. Many people view the three-fifths compromise as a way of making slaves less than whole people. Frederick Douglass held that opinion but changed his mind after winning his freedom. Douglass was an African American, a US official, and a prominent author in the 1800s, and he had escaped from slavery. "My new circumstances, compelled me to rethink the whole subject. . . . I was conducted to the conclusion that the Constitution of the United States . . . not only contained no guarantees in favor of slavery, but, on the contrary was in its letter and spirit an anti-slavery instrument."[8]

Douglass saw in the three-fifths compromise an effort by antislavery Northerners to reduce the power of the South and eventually abolish slavery throughout the country. But slavery remained a topic of hot debate and legal wrangling for decades after the Constitutional Convention. The issue would continue to divide the nation, fracturing the union sought by the framers of the Constitution into a country split into two unbending, hostile camps. There would be more compromises, but legal slavery did not end until the conclusion of the Civil War in 1865.

DISCUSSION STARTERS

- Why do you think so many people in the 1700s were comfortable with enslaving black people?

- Why do you think most slaves in Virginia did not try to escape and flee to the North?

- What do you think of the three-fifths compromise?

CHAPTER FOUR

SLAVERY, TRADE, AND POLITICS

A round the time of the Constitutional Convention, Northern states began abolishing slavery. The Northwest Ordinance of 1787 banned slavery in the Northwest Territory, which later became Illinois, Indiana, Michigan, Ohio, and Wisconsin. This law laid the groundwork for the division of the country into slave states and free states.

Seeing slavery as vital to their economic growth, Southern states held fast to the institution. But abolition by law or by a phrase in a state constitution did not necessarily mean that slavery ended, even in the North. Some Northerners

White landowners in the South benefited greatly by enslaving people and forcing them to work.

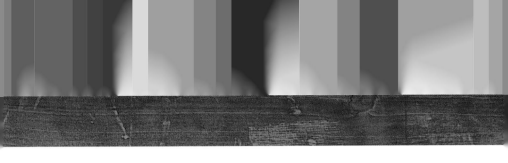

BANNING SLAVERY IN THE NORTH

By the time of the Constitutional Convention in 1787, several Northern states had banned slavery. Vermont became the first in 1777. Pennsylvania followed in 1780, New Hampshire and Massachusetts in 1783, and Rhode Island in 1784. However, despite these legal bans, actual laws punishing the ownership or sale of slaves were scarce.

For example, many residents of Vermont continued to employ unpaid "servants" and apprentices who were not free to seek other employment, or even move out of their households. In addition, free blacks were kidnapped within the state's borders, and runaways were captured and returned to their owners. Slavery by another name survived in many "free" states of the North. By the time of the Civil War, involuntary servitude was dying out as the abolitionist movement gained steam in New England and elsewhere in the North.

continued to use unpaid "servants," forcing them to labor without wages. In addition, several Northern states passed fugitive slave laws, which made sheltering runaway slaves a crime. And because the Constitution put off a ban on the slave trade until 1808, lawmakers in Congress saw no need to write new federal laws about slavery.

So legal slavery continued throughout the South, while Northern politicians remained silent on the practice of slavery in their own states. The attention of Congress in the early 1800s was on the westward expansion of the country's borders. For example, the federal government established territories covering millions of acres of land for settlement west of Georgia, in a vast region then known as the Yazoo. Hopeful farmers and settlers bought this land. Eventually, the Yazoo would become the states of Alabama and Mississippi.

The land rush was set off by the promise of fertile soil for rice, indigo, sugarcane, and cotton. These crops could only be raised on a large scale with the use of slave labor. The export of these products to Europe brought money and foreign investment into the US economy. While Southern planters relied on slave labor, Northern shipowners also benefited directly from the trade in slaves and, after the import of slaves was banned, by the shipment

OMINOUS WARNINGS

Although politicians in the late 1700s disagreed on many things, many were united in promoting or at least tolerating slavery. But even for many early political leaders in the United States, this stark division between free and slave-owning states boded very ill for the nation's future. Reflecting on slavery in *Notes on the State of Virginia*, Thomas Jefferson wrote, "I tremble for my country when I reflect that God is just."[1] And politician George Mason wrote in 1787, "[Slaves] bring the judgment of heaven on a country. As nations cannot be rewarded or punished in the next world, they must be in this. By an inevitable chain of causes and effects, providence punishes national sins, by national calamities."[2] Many historians see in this statement a prophecy of the worst calamity to ever befall the United States: the Civil War.

of Southern cash crops to European markets. New York merchants profited from the sale of cotton, and New England textile mills relied on the same product as a raw material. Slave-based agriculture supported an expanding system of banking and credit—the foundation of the national economy.

This was a key reason why Northern politicians agreed to oppose a proposed law banning slavery in the Yazoo territory. This decision, among others, put off the issue of banning slavery in new territories west of the Mississippi River.

Slavery and Credit

Land, in the Yazoo region and elsewhere, was seen by many people as one of the country's few worthwhile investments. In the nation's early years, money was scarce. The government issued paper currency that held little value. Barter exchange was common, and on the frontier, people exchanged common items such as deerskins as a form of currency.

Credit and a banking system were crucial to correct the serious shortage of money and to allow businesses and the economy to grow. People who were enslaved entered the calculation as collateral for loans. They were seen as a form of personal property, and they could be bought and sold by their slaveholders. If a farmer sought to buy more

Enslaved people were at the mercy of the slaveholders and had no rights.

A Deal in Baton Rouge

No matter his own race, a slaveholder could put up other human beings as collateral. In their book *Slavery's Capitalism*, historians Sven Beckert and Seth Rockman explain that the exchange of slaves was common among "free persons of color" in Louisiana. In Baton Rouge, Louisiana, Juan Bautista Massi, who had both white and black ancestry, purchased three female slaves from Armand Duplantier in 1803. Duplantier had set a price of 1,800 Mexican pesos. Lacking the cash, Massi pledged five slaves he already owned, as well as the three he was purchasing.[3] He would be bound to turn the collateral over to Duplantier if he should fail to eventually pay the money.

land and needed to borrow money, he also needed to put up collateral that a lender could seize in case the loan was not repaid.

Banks and lenders throughout the country accepted slaves as collateral for loans. The value of enslaved people was relatively high compared with other items such as horses, wagons, and farming tools. The law set no limit or restrictions on the use of slaves in this way, and the practice occurred with no regard to the slaves or their ties to a home or family. It was common to separate children from parents, or husbands from wives, and to tear families apart when the terms of a business deal called for the transfer of an enslaved person from one slaveholder to another.

Using slaves as collateral helped the development of the money-scarce frontier west of the Mississippi River.

It allowed settlers to buy land where they could plant crops and raise animals. It also allowed farmers to invest in tools, livestock, seeds, and more land. Owning more land allowed more-efficient production of cash crops and higher income for the white landowners. Higher income allowed slaveholders to buy even more slaves and build small farms into large plantations. This growth spurred the building of new banks and market centers, where businesses bought and sold commodities grown in the countryside. The frontier steadily advanced westward, supported by the credit system in which the exchange of slaves played a key role.

SLAVERY AND DEVELOPMENT

The purchase of frontier land, which depended on credit and loans, was necessary for new states to become viable and for the nation to reach the Mississippi River valley. However, in the early 1800s, ownership of the territory beyond the Mississippi was still in doubt. The English, French, and Spanish still had claims on western territories and the land now covered by Minnesota, Iowa, Missouri, Arkansas, and Texas.

In the general view of Northerners, banning or opposing slavery in the region would harm the interests of the United States. It would discourage settlement and development of the region, allowing rival nations to conquer a valuable swath of territory. This, in turn, would thwart the development of the United States as a continental power. Jefferson agreed with various arguments for keeping slavery, and the practice remained legal in the Yazoo territory.

RHODE ISLAND AND THE SLAVE TRADE

In the Northeast, opposition to slavery gathered steam in the 1700s. One of the strongest factions in this movement

DECIDING FOR SLAVERY

The Yazoo land rush began when the empire of Spain surrendered its claims to land west of Georgia in 1795. In the same year, speculators bribed members of the Georgia legislature to sell millions of acres of land to four different land investment companies for $500,000.[4] These firms then sold their land to other companies that broke up the territory into smaller claims and sold these parcels to individual speculators and ambitious cash-crop farmers. Many slaves from the Virginia area were sold and forced to march to the Yazoo for service on the new plantations.

The next year, Georgia's lawmakers decided that the state had been robbed by an illegal contract. They declared the 1795 sale null and void. The dispute was not resolved until the US Supreme Court decision in the 1810 case of *Fletcher v. Peck*. This decision laid down the principle that business contracts had to be honored, even if they were secured by an illegal act such as bribery. As a result of this decision, it would be easier for slaveholders to keep slaves as personal property, regardless of any laws a state or federal government passed against the institution, no matter where the slave was located, and no matter the terms and conditions of the sale.

was a religious group called the Society of Friends, also known as the Quakers. In Rhode Island, most Quaker congregations banned slavery among their members by the time of the Revolutionary War. In 1784, Rhode Island passed a law to gradually emancipate slaves. Adult slaves remained enslaved, but children born to them were now called apprentices. When girls reached the age of 18 and boys 21, they would gain their freedom.

The Quakers had a powerful opponent in the Rhode Island shipping business. Rhode Island ships had long been major players in the slave trade. By one estimate, Rhode Island ships had carried more than 100,000 Africans to North America as slaves by 1808—the year the transatlantic slave trade ended. And more than 60 percent of slave-trading voyages from North America during this time set out from Rhode Island.[5]

A 1787 Rhode Island law banned residents from trading slaves, although traders continued to run illegal slaving voyages from the state's ports. Federal laws in 1794 and 1800 banned Americans from transporting slaves to foreign countries. Even after Congress abolished the transatlantic slave trade throughout the country in 1808, slaves were bought, sold, and moved by Rhode Islanders and others in the years following the ban.

The transatlantic slave trade carried millions of captured Africans to the Americas.

SLAVERY'S CONTRIBUTIONS

The trade in slaves and other goods made Newport one of the wealthiest cities in the country. Many institutions prominent in Rhode Island history directly benefited from slavery. One of these was Brown University, founded in Providence, Rhode Island, in 1764. Members of the Brown family, for whom the university was named, were important figures in the transport of slaves. And the university's first president, Reverend James Manning, was himself a slaveholder.

Universities in Virginia and throughout the South were built with slave labor and were lent financial support by slaveholders. In the 2000s, many of these institutions began exploring this shadowy side of their histories. Brown University, the University of Virginia, and Duke University have all carried out projects that look into their connections to slavery and how slaves contributed to their founding and growth. Some have even created memorials recognizing their connection to slavery. For example, Brown University has a sculpture relating to the transatlantic slave trade—a trade that the university benefited from. The sculpture is of a broken chain connected to a mostly buried ball, which represents a history that's both heavy and partly buried.

DISCUSSION STARTERS

- Many politicians in the 1700s supported slavery because the practice benefited them personally. Do you think today's politicians do the same thing, but with different practices? Explain your answer.

- Thomas Jefferson once wrote about the ill effects of slavery on those who held slaves. Why do you think Jefferson himself would remain a slaveholder, even though he held these opinions?

- Many cities and universities are exploring their historic connections to slavery. Do you think this is worthwhile? Explain your answer.

CHAPTER FIVE

THE COTTON ECONOMY

I n the 1700s, slave-grown cotton in South America and the West Indies fueled Britain's Industrial Revolution, which was a rapid industry development caused by new machinery. New machinery used in the textile industry produced a vast amount of fabric and finished clothing, making these goods increasingly affordable. As wages and productivity rose, a consumer-driven economy was born. A new class of factory workers was employed to operate the technology to make textile products.

Britain needed cotton as a vital raw material. But farmers could not produce cotton locally, because cotton plants could not survive in the British soil and climate. Cotton had to come from

Cotton was a massive industry in the South. The industry's success was made possible by enslaved labor.

Enslaved labor helped plantation owners grow more crops.

warmer regions, where slaves were necessary for the work
of planting, cultivating, and harvesting the crop. However,
the growing demand for cotton still posed a problem:
there was a limited quantity of cultivable land in areas
where cotton competed with other valuable cash crops
such as sugar, rice, and indigo.

The newly annexed territories of the American South
offered a solution: a vast new territory of uncultivated
and fertile soil. The first cotton in the United States
was planted on the Sea Islands off the Georgia coast in
1786. As the international demand for cotton grew, the

price of Southern growing land increased. In the late 1700s, speculators sent land prices skyrocketing in the unorganized territories west of Georgia.

Eventually, the so-called cotton belt would stretch a thousand miles to the west, beyond the Mississippi River, into Arkansas, Louisiana, and Texas. But at the onset of the 1800s, the ownership of this trans-Mississippi region remained in doubt, even with the Louisiana Purchase of 1803, in which France sold millions of acres west of the Mississippi to the United States. During the War of 1812 (1812–1815), the British contested US ownership of the lower Mississippi. The defeat of a British army at New Orleans in 1815 put an end to Britain's claim. This ensured that a slave-based economy firmly under American control would prevail in what is now Louisiana, Arkansas, and Texas.

In the early 1800s, the cotton economy was growing in the South. The invention of the cotton gin in the 1790s automated the laborious process of cleaning seeds from harvested cotton bolls. Using a cotton gin, a worker could clean the harvested bolls 50 times faster than when doing it by hand. However, farmers soon discovered that growing cotton quickly depleted the soil. In search of fertile land, they continually moved west, bringing along their slaves.

The Cotton Boom

Slavery was essential to land speculation and rising cotton production in the South. As Britain's demand for raw cotton increased, prices for cotton rose. As the cotton boom intensified in the early 1830s, cotton farmers saw no end to the demand for their crop. Banks throughout the country and from overseas got into the business. Bankers extended credit to borrowers on the expectation that the value of their collateral—cotton, land, and slaves—would continue to increase.

In this economy, many people feared being left behind. The cotton belt in the South became the destination for many young men who sought their fortunes. One of them was a Virginia lawyer named Joseph Baldwin, who in 1836 struck out for Mississippi. In a memoir he

The Reinvention of Slavery

A single invention, Eli Whitney's cotton gin, prompted the rapid growth of the US cotton industry. Invented in 1793, the device allowed slaves to clean cotton of its seeds faster than they could by hand. The cotton gin also revived slavery at a time when the slave trade was beginning to decline. This falloff in slave trading was one reason why the nation's founders assumed the issue would eventually disappear and a ban on the slave trade could be put off for 20 years. As the demand for cotton skyrocketed, the demand for slaves also rose. The transatlantic slave trade was thriving when it was banned by an act of Congress that took effect in 1808.

wrote later, Baldwin said, "The new country seemed to be a reservoir, and every road leading to it a vagrant stream of enterprise and adventure."[1]

Over the years, cotton production increased because of a cruel system forced upon slave laborers. Cotton pickers were subject to a daily quota, in pounds, on the amount of cotton they had to gather. Missing that quota meant a beating, a lashing, or some other form of torture. Over the years and generations, under the threat of that punishment, the dexterity and speed of cotton pickers—many of whom were women and children—increased.

Holding slaves was the key to a profitable cotton operation. The more slaves a person had, the more

MODERN COTTON

Today, the cotton economy has survived, although it has gone through major changes since the 1800s. Growing cotton is now almost completely mechanized, with diesel-powered combines and other machinery available for planting, cultivating, and harvesting. Although the Mississippi delta still grows most of the country's cotton, production has shifted to Texas and other western states, including Arizona and California. In 2017 and 2018, the United States was the third largest producer of cotton after India and China. But the target countries for exports are no longer in Europe. Instead, textile and clothing production has shifted to Asia, especially developing countries such as Bangladesh and Malaysia, where wages are much lower than in Europe or the United States.

Enslaved people were forced to pick a certain amount of cotton each day.

he could earn, and the more money he could borrow. In Mississippi, cotton production totaled 85 million pounds (39 million kg) in 1834. It rose to 125 million pounds (57 million kg) in 1836 and to 200 million pounds (91 million kg) in 1839. This was one quarter of all the cotton produced in the United States.[2]

Mississippi banned the importation of slaves into the state as merchandise or for sale in 1833. Cotton planters got around the law by buying slaves outside of the state and bringing them in under the guise of personal servants, which were explicitly allowed by the new law. In addition, Mississippi continued to tax the sale of slaves, gathering money from an activity that it had already deemed illegal but conveniently overlooked.

THE COTTON BUST

The cotton boom ended when prices began to fall in 1836. By early 1837, the cotton economy was in a meltdown. As cotton prices continued to decline, so did the value of land and of slaves. With their revenues falling, cotton farmers found they were unable to repay their debts. Land buyers disappeared, and many farms were simply abandoned by bankrupt owners, many of whom left everything behind except their slaves.

The cotton-based economy of the South recovered over the following decades. By the Civil War, the

Britain and the Confederacy

By the early 1800s, Britain's textile industry was dependent on slave-grown cotton from the US South, which had surpassed the West Indies and South America in cotton production. Many historians have pointed out that the Industrial Revolution, which began in English textile mills, could not have taken place without the slave-based farming economy of the southern United States. For this reason, many British people sided with the Confederacy during the Civil War, even though the government was officially neutral and slavery was officially banned throughout the British Empire in 1833.

To keep up the transatlantic shipment of cotton bales during the war, the British sent blockade-running ships to pass through the barrier of Union warships that was preventing trade through Southern ports. The British brought arms, clothing, food, and other materials that kept the Confederacy alive for four long years of war.

cotton-growing South was among the world's richest agricultural regions and the wealthiest section of the United States. The industry also kept the United States at peace with Europe, where textile industries depended on the plentiful supply of high-grade cotton from the United States. In 1858, Senator James Henry Hammond of South Carolina asked, "Would any sane nation make war on cotton? . . . . No power on earth dares to make war upon it. Cotton is King."[3] Cotton remained the principal export of the United States until the 1930s.

However, the pre–Civil War cotton economy was built on slave labor. This was why President Abraham

Lincoln's opposition to slavery was resisted, to the point of secession, by the Southern states. "The all-encompassing control of workers—a core characteristic of capitalism—experienced its first great success on the cotton plantations of the American South," writes historian Sven Beckert in his book *Empire of Cotton*.[4] In the decades following the Civil War, some industries controlled and organized their workers on a massive scale, following the example of Southern cotton plantations. This was a key ingredient of the rapid postwar industrialization that transformed the United States into a global economic power.

DISCUSSION STARTERS

- The South relied on slaves to do demanding labor to keep the area's cotton economy thriving. Has the United States ever relied on other groups of people to do hard labor in unfair working conditions? Explain your answer.

- How do you think enslaved people felt when they were forced to pick a certain amount of cotton each day?

- Do you think it was smart for the South's economy to rely on certain cash crops, such as cotton? Explain your answer.

CHAPTER SIX

MAKING A BREADBASKET

It was a warm July day in 1831, in the Shenandoah Valley of western Virginia— harvest time in the fields of tall, ripened wheat. Near one of these fields, a group of friends and neighbors stood alongside inventor Cyrus McCormick and a man he enslaved, Jo Anderson. In front of them stood a strange contraption. It had a large, circular reel, a set of cutting bars, a wooden platform, and a small footplate for a man to stand on. A horse stood in front, ready to pull the machine.

At a signal, the horse began walking forward. The reel on the contraption began to turn. The sharp cutting bars sliced through the wheat stalks. The blades swept the wheat onto the platform.

The McCormick reaper reduced the number of laborers needed to harvest wheat.

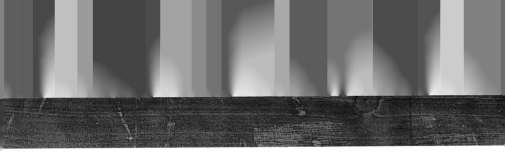

The men standing alongside the field watched with great curiosity. If this strange machine actually worked, and did what McCormick promised, it would mean a revolution for wheat-growing farmers.

THE ARDUOUS TASK

McCormick and other Virginia wheat farmers depended on slaves to plant, cultivate, and harvest their crops. Wheat, like cotton and tobacco, was a labor-intensive crop. Farmers needed large crews of slaves to cut the ripe wheat stalks, bundle the stalks into shocks to dry, and separate the chaff from the grain that could be milled into flour.

At harvest time, everybody worked long and hard days. If the wheat was cut too early, it would be of lower quality. But if it was cut too late, the wheat was subject to mold and rot. Demand for flour was high in distant, slave-owning Brazil—the principal export market for Virginia flour. The faster a wheat farmer could get his good-quality product to the mills, the more he would earn for it.

At one time, small mills built alongside streams and rivers milled most wheat in Virginia. Farmers did not have to bring their crop very far, and they had a dependable local wheat market. But in the early 1800s, the milling industry went through a change. Large company-owned

Cyrus McCormick continued to improve the reaper as time went on.

COFFEE IN BRAZIL

Brazil's coffee economy paralleled the cotton kingdom of the US South. In the early 1800s, slave-grown coffee imported from southeastern Brazil became the global beverage of choice, replacing the tea imported from around the world by the English. In the United States, coffee was considered a more acceptable drug than tobacco or alcohol. In addition, the Industrial Revolution created a need for hardworking factory employees who would arrive early, stay long hours, and remain as wakeful as possible. The caffeine in coffee could help with this.

mills were set up in Richmond, Virginia—a city on the James River. Oceangoing ships began transporting Richmond flour to Brazil.

GIFTING A PERSON

Supplying wheat flour to Brazil meant farmers had to get their crop in as quickly as possible. They also had to get it to market fast, as wheat easily spoiled during transportation. Wheat farmers were now in a faster, more competitive business—and the old way of planting and harvesting wheat by manual labor would have to change. Anderson helped bring this change about.

Although Cyrus McCormick has received the credit for the mechanical reaper, Anderson made essential contributions. He was born in 1808 at Walnut Grove, the McCormick family plantation. Robert, the father of Cyrus

McCormick, gave Anderson to his son as a gift, and the two boys grew up together. McCormick and Anderson worked together on a simple mechanical reaper. And together, they introduced the improved reaper at the field near Steeles Tavern, Virginia, in 1831. While the machine moved down the rows, Anderson walked alongside, raking the wheat stalks from the reaper's platform and onto the ground behind.

Rebellion and Law

In Virginia's Southampton County, Nat Turner, a slave, started a rebellion in 1831 that sparked fear among slaveholders and white citizens throughout the South. The rebellion resulted in the deaths of more than 50 whites and about a dozen slaves, and Turner himself was captured, tortured, and executed.[1] The fear of slave uprisings brought about new laws that banned education for slaves as well as for free blacks. This was a precursor to the laws restricting civil and voting rights for freedmen after the Civil War.

African American Inventors

As an enslaved person, Anderson could not start a business or apply for a patent on an invention. Those rights belonged to free men such as McCormick, who received a patent on the reaper in 1834. To reach a wider market, McCormick moved in 1846 to Chicago, Illinois, where he started a company and set up a factory.

The McCormick reaper became a familiar sight in the wheat fields of the Midwest. These new states became

BLEEDING IN KANSAS

Congress struggled with the issue of slavery as the country's frontier moved west. In 1854, the Kansas–Nebraska Act decreed that the voters in each new state would decide whether to have slavery. A rush of proslavery men flooded into Kansas, determined to extend slavery's reach westward. This set off a series of bitter fights known as Bleeding Kansas, with raids and massacres becoming common occurrences between proslavery and antislavery backers in the years just before the Civil War.

This conflict over slavery gave prominence to John Brown, who fought against the proslavery faction in Kansas. A few years later, Brown would lead a group of men in a raid on a federal arsenal. His intention was to spark a slave uprising, but he was defeated, captured, and later executed for the raid, becoming a martyr to the abolitionist cause. Another prominent fighter on slavery's western frontier was Jesse James, who joined private militias on the proslavery side in Missouri and later became the nation's best-known bank robber.

a vast breadbasket of productive small farms, worked without slave labor. McCormick found business success, fame, and wealth. He also remained a strong proslavery man and a supporter of the Confederacy even after moving to the free state of Illinois.

In the meantime, Anderson remained in Virginia. McCormick gave Anderson his freedom before the Civil War. Unable to earn a living on his own, Anderson hired himself out as a laborer at the rate of $60 to $70 each year—money his employers paid to McCormick.[2] McCormick allowed Anderson to continue living on the

The Midwest has millions of acres of land that are used for agriculture.

McCormick property and paid Anderson a small allowance out of the money Anderson earned.

History has overlooked Anderson and other African Americans for the part they played in different inventions and innovations. Henry Boyd of Kentucky invented a new kind of bed. Benjamin Montgomery invented a propeller for a steamboat that would work in shallow water. Thomas Jennings invented the process of dry cleaning. As a free

Thomas Jennings bought his family out of slavery after he got money from his patent.

black man, Jennings was granted a patent in 1821—
the first African American to win legal protection for
his invention.

After the Civil War, the McCormick reaper
transformed the Midwest into the nation's breadbasket—a
region of productive farms that provided the bulk of the
country's food supply. The McCormick company was
merged into International Harvester (IH) in 1902. Like
many other older US companies, IH was established with
major contributions from slavery and slaveholders.

DISCUSSION STARTERS

- Has your education taught you about African American inventors? If yes, what have you learned? If no, why do you think that is?

- Why do you think history focuses so much on the contributions of white men and not on other groups of people?

- Do you think it's fair to not get recognition for the work you've done? Explain your answer.

CHAPTER SEVEN

THE CIVIL WAR AND ITS AFTERMATH

The Civil War erupted in 1861. The issues of slavery and the right to own slaves divided the North and South. The Southern states believed they had the right to decide whether to have slavery. This states' rights idea set them at odds with the federal government and its authority to set down the law on slavery and other matters.

After the election of President Lincoln in 1860, Southern leaders began fearing a federal ban on slavery. Lincoln, in fact, did not call for national abolition of slavery. At the time, he only officially opposed slavery in newly organized states and territories.

The Civil War was the deadliest conflict in US history.

Nevertheless, 11 Southern states declared their independence from the United States after Lincoln became president. They organized a Confederate States of America with its own president, capital city, and legislature. Determined to hold the country together, Lincoln decided to go to war. The spark that set off the conflict was a bombardment by Confederate forces of Fort Sumter, held by the US army in the harbor of Charleston, South Carolina.

The Civil War continued for four years, ending with the defeat of the Confederacy in April 1865. The Southern states were returned, by force, to the Union. Slavery was banned by the Thirteenth Amendment to the Constitution. This created a large population of newly freed African Americans in the South. The issue of their rights, and the reconstruction of the South's laws and economy, occupied the US government for decades and has echoes in modern-day politics.

CIVIL WAR AMENDMENTS

Important changes to the legal system addressed the problem of slavery and the newly emancipated slaves. The Fourteenth Amendment established citizenship for all persons born in the United States. This meant African Americans were now full citizens with the right to

Southern forces attacked Fort Sumter after they seceded from the Union.

"equal protection" of the law.[1] In addition, the Fifteenth Amendment gave African American men the right to vote.

The former states of the Confederacy had to ratify these amendments before the federal government admitted them back into the Union. Gradually they did so, with Georgia rejoining last in 1870.

In the same way slavery helped build the US economy, the Civil War amendments laid the foundation of the country's modern legal system. In theory, any law can be challenged on constitutional grounds. This means

OPPOSING THE THIRTEENTH

The Thirteenth Amendment banned legal slavery in the United States, but its interpretation is still the subject of controversy. The amendment reads: "Neither slavery nor involuntary servitude, except as a punishment for crime whereof the party shall have been duly convicted, shall exist within the United States, or any place subject to their jurisdiction."[2]

Some people oppose the Thirteenth Amendment on the grounds that it grants state and federal prisons the constitutional right to enslave American citizens. As an example, they point to the use of unpaid, or nearly unpaid, prison labor—a reminder of the days when African Americans were forced to work for nothing. For some observers, the Thirteenth Amendment was a way to deliberately keep African Americans enslaved through the criminal justice system, as blacks still make up a large percentage of inmates in federal prisons.

that any state or city that passes a law must follow the principles laid down by the Constitution and its amendments. For example, the justices of the Supreme Court have referenced the Fourteenth Amendment's equal protection clause thousands of times in their decisions. Equal protection means every person in the United States has the same legal rights as everyone else. In this way, the principles of equal civil rights, the right to vote, the right to defend oneself in court against criminal charges, and the rights of citizenship all trace their origins to the institution of slavery and its aftermath.

Reconstruction

The Reconstruction era began with the liberation of four million slaves.[3] The federal government established a new agency known as the Freedmen's Bureau. This group helped liberated slaves buy property, establish businesses, and gain education and job training. The United States also sent its military into the Southern states as an occupying force. Some Southern farms were seized and parceled out to the freedmen. African American men won elections to Southern legislatures, as well as to the US Congress. Southern states passed laws guaranteeing equal access to education, public accommodations, and transport.

Southerners who were opposed to Reconstruction fought back by enacting laws known as Black Codes that restricted the rights of African Americans to vote, own a business, get an education, and use public facilities. Some of the Black

Modern Slavery

Although the United States no longer allows slavery, the practice is still seen in other parts of the world. The Walk Free Foundation, a group that works to end slavery around the globe, estimated that 29.8 million people were enslaved in 2013, with the number rising to 45.8 million in 2016.[4] In 2011, California became the first state to address the issue with the California Transparency in Supply Chains Act. Companies in the state had to show their attempts to stop buying goods from abroad made with forced labor.

Codes were declared illegal by the federal government and by military governors in the South. But others were revived after the end of Reconstruction in 1877.

After the end of the Civil War, Confederate war veterans organized the Ku Klux Klan (KKK) to oppose federal Reconstruction policies. The KKK has survived, in one form or another, into the present day. The group used threats, violence, and murder to intimidate African Americans who were claiming their legal rights and white people who accepted integration.

The discussion of states' rights was an important legacy of Reconstruction. Opposition to federal policies, and the powers of the federal government in general, became a mainstay of Southern and conservative politicians. These leaders did not suggest or support a return to legalized slavery. But they did claim to advance the original intent of the Constitution—a balance of powers that left the responsibility for deciding civil rights largely with the individual states.

SHARECROPPING

The Civil War caused widespread destruction in the South. Homes, shops, factories, railroads, and farms were destroyed. Without slave labor to power trade and agriculture, the Southern economy went into a tailspin. Once the most prosperous section of the country, it

The KKK wanted to restrict African Americans from taking part in public life.

became the poorest in the years after the war, and remains so today.

The cotton economy remained significant. But the slavery-based plantation system came to an end. Freedmen trying to establish their own farms ran into laws and customs that prevented them from buying land. They were hard-pressed to get loans or other support from banks or the government to buy homes, land, or essential equipment.

Textbooks and Slavery

Textbooks created a century after slavery was abolished published inaccurate information about how slaves lived. In a history book used in Virginia until the 1970s, the writer claims that slaveholders "managed their servants according to their own methods. They knew the best way to control their slaves was to win their confidence and affection." For this reason, the text continues, "Many Negroes were taught to read and write. Many of them were allowed to meet in groups for preaching, for funerals, and for singing and dancing. They went visiting at night and sometimes owned guns and other weapons."[5]

This history reflects a view once common in the South—that slaveholders did the best for their slaves by offering them shelter and food, and therefore slavery was not so bad. This view of slavery as a benign institution in schoolbooks of the South is still a subject of controversy in the field of education.

Instead, a system of labor contracts engaged them to work at low wages for plantation owners. Over the years, a system of sharecropping also emerged in the South. Black families lived on farming estates as tenants rather than owners. They grew crops and paid their rent with a share of the harvest each year. For tools, seeds, and other essentials, they depended on merchants who advanced these goods on credit and kept their customers in lifelong debt.

In 1873, a financial panic swept the country. Many banks failed, unemployment rose, and businesses closed their doors. With their attention on economic issues, politicians from the North turned their attention away from the problems of the freedmen. In the South, state legislatures began passing new laws that didn't always conform to the Constitution as amended after the Civil War. This brought about new battles over civil and voting rights, and new divisions in the country that have continued to the present day.

Discussion Starters

- Do you think the federal government should be able to tell states what to do? Explain your answer.

- The idea of states' rights is still a hot issue in US politics. The Supreme Court has struck down many state laws as unconstitutional. Do you think the court should have the authority to do that? Explain your reasoning.

- During Reconstruction, federal armies occupied the former Confederate states and military governors ran them. What do you think would have happened in the South without military occupation?

CONFEDERATE SYMBOLS TODAY

Although the Confederacy lost the Civil War, its flag survived. Several Southern states incorporated it in their own state flags. The Confederate flag even flew in front of government buildings. The flag came to symbolize the traditional South, including the segregation of the races. It also took on a new meaning for white supremacist hate groups such as the KKK, which was founded on the idea that freed slaves should stay at the bottom of the social and economic ladder.

The flag also reemerged as a popular symbol during the civil rights movement in the 1950s and 1960s. Historian David Goldfield, who wrote *Still Fighting the Civil War*, said, "In 1962, the state of South Carolina put the Confederate battle flag atop the capitol building in Columbia, South Carolina. The public reason for that [was that they] were celebrating the 100th anniversary of the Civil War. But in fact it was again a flag of defiance [against] the federal government and racial equality, because it was at the height of the Civil Rights Movement in the South."[6]

Other symbols of the Confederacy, including statues of Southern military heroes such as General Robert E. Lee and even the names of streets and highways, have become the focus of controversy. That's because many people view these as symbols of white supremacy. In the 2000s, some city and state governments chose to take down Confederate symbols that were in public spaces. For example, in 2017, New Orleans took down Confederate monuments that celebrated Civil War leaders such as Confederate president Jefferson Davis.

The Confederate flag at South Carolina's capitol building was eventually taken down in 2015.

CHAPTER EIGHT

RECONSTRUCTION AND MODERN AMERICA

After the US economy recovered from the panic of 1873, it began growing again. A vast western frontier opened up to settlers and farmers. Many former slaves joined this great exodus to the west as cowboys, ranchers, miners, or soldiers.

The miserable conditions faced by many African Americans in the South remained. The federal government's support for the well-being and legal rights of black people largely vanished after Reconstruction. The system of sharecropping trapped generations of families in poverty and debt.

Southern leaders, determined to maintain the traditional economic privileges of whites, saw to

The sharecropping system was essentially another form of enslavement for African Americans.

it that African Americans were kept in an inferior place. Segregation laws kept the children of black families in separate schools. Private businesses such as hotels and restaurants also enforced segregation. Blacks found themselves kept out altogether or forced to stay or eat in separate facilities.

Many African Americans moved north. Factory jobs drew many to large cities such as New York City and Chicago, as well as Cleveland, Ohio, and Detroit, Michigan. Life was generally better when a worker could earn dependable wages, even if the wages were low. Factory jobs were better than simply working a field of crops for the temporary right to live on the farm and going hungry if the crops failed.

South and North

Industrialization was transforming big cities in the East and Midwest. In the late 1800s, Northern factories were making goods on a massive scale—everything from nails to shoes to steam boilers. Large corporations were forming, hiring employees, and growing. In some industries, monopolies were forming. A single company or small group of companies dominated major economic sectors such as oil, sugar, steel, and tobacco.

While the North experienced rapid industrial and commercial growth, the South fell behind. The Civil War

Some African Americans in the late 1800s worked at laundries.

had inflicted massive damage on many Southern cities. The end of slavery and the movement of African Americans to the North depleted the Southern labor force. In addition, drawn by factory jobs, immigrants from Europe were settling in Northern cities rather than Southern ones.

Cultural attitudes may have also played a part in the economic decline of the South. Historians have argued that white Southerners avoided manual labor, associating it with slavery. Most manufacturing companies were slow to establish themselves in the South. Farming continued to dominate Southern economic life. But farming, including growing cotton, was subject to low profit margins, falling crop prices, weak export markets, and the changing value of land. All of these factors make farming an uncertain business in any region.

Even 150 years after the Civil War, the South still lagged behind the northern, midwestern, and western sections of the United States. A US Census Bureau survey of 2016 revealed that incomes and industrial production were lower and the poverty rate higher in the South. In 2008, the United States went through a deep recession. The economy declined and many banks failed. The recession saw the South experience the nation's biggest increases in families living in poverty. Although many factors contribute to these problems, slavery and the war that ended it still cast a long shadow over the region.

History and Legacy

Legal slavery was stopped by the Thirteenth Amendment. With the end of the Civil War, the issue of abolitionist versus slaveholder seemed to be decided once and for all. But many companies that survived the war and continued to grow had a connection to slavery. This connection still raised problems for these companies in the 2000s.

For example, the insurance company Aetna was established shortly before the Civil War. In those years, the

PEOPLE LIVING IN POVERTY, 2017[2]

The US Census Bureau published 2017 data showing that poverty is not distributed equally throughout the United States.

company sold insurance policies on the lives of slaves. By buying such a policy, a slaveholder was reimbursed when one of the slaves covered by the policy died. "Aetna has long acknowledged that for several years . . . the company may have insured the lives of slaves," commented a spokesman in 2000. "We express our deep regret over any participation at all in this deplorable practice."[1]

The railroad company CSX also faces the issue of its connection to slavery. Southern railroads that later merged into CSX used slave labor to build their track. The railroads rented these slaves for up to $200 a season for their work—money that was paid to the slaveholders.[3]

This history has inspired lawsuits and petitions seeking reparations for slavery. Modern descendants of slaves are seeking damages in court or through legislatures for harms and unpaid labor. One lawsuit was filed by plaintiff Deadria Farmer-Paellmann and others in 2002 against Aetna, CSX, and other companies. These reparations, in the view of the plaintiffs, were owed to descendants of slaves. However, as of 2018 the defending companies have given only formal apologies for their history.

By calculations made in 2014 by Larry Neal, an economist at the University of Illinois, the value of wages lost by slaves between 1620 and 1840, in modern money and with interest, is more than $6.5 trillion.[4]

PRESENT-DAY SLAVERY

Several companies doing business in the United States still rely on slave labor or laborers forced to work in terrible conditions to produce their goods. For example, in 2009, Nestlé, a food and drink company, was sued by some child slaves from Africa. These children claimed they were forced into harvesting cocoa.

Other companies associated with forced labor or very poorly paid foreign labor include Nike, Starbucks, and Walmart. And within the United States, companies that have relied on prison laborers include Whole Foods, McDonald's, AT&T, and Victoria's Secret.

Opponents of reparations claim that with no living slaves, nobody now living has any claim of damages for slavery. But supporters say it's about righting a wrong. "Reparations are not simply about money; they represent the acknowledgment of a wrong and a material effort to make it right," wrote author Marianne Williamson in the *Washington Post*. "They are about dignity and respect."[5]

DISCUSSION STARTERS

- Do you think the descendants of slaves should be repaid for the unpaid labor of their ancestors? Explain your answer.

- Many companies operating today have ties to slavery. Do you think their leaders should apologize for this history?

- How would you feel if you were segregated from others based on a physical quality you have?

CHAPTER NINE

ENDURING RACISM

At the time of the Civil War, Oklahoma was Indian Territory—a place the federal government reserved for Native Americans who were forced from their lands in the South. There never was legal slavery in Oklahoma, as there was in neighboring Texas and Arkansas. There were no plantations, and the climate and soil were not right for cotton or other cash crops.

But there was a land rush on Oklahoma's plains after oil was discovered in 1901 near Tulsa. The city prospered from the oil boom, and black families moved in—most of them from the South. They lived in the bustling Greenwood neighborhood, where black owners ran restaurants, shops, a theater, and other businesses.

The Tulsa riot destroyed the possessions of many African American people.

Underneath the city's prosperity was resentment. African Americans doing well was a perceived problem for many whites. White people who moved to Oklahoma from other Southern states brought notions of white racial supremacy. Their mind-set was a legacy of the slavery era. Above all, according to these traditional racist ideas, there would be no interracial marriage or dating, or even friendly interactions, between black men and white women.

ONE OF MANY RIOTS

Race riots took place with frequency in the years after World War I (1914–1918). African Americans staking a claim to an equal place and equal rights fueled anger among some whites who had a very different notion of what African Americans' place should be. These beliefs were drawn from the era of slavery. During the summer of 1919, there were deadly riots in Chicago; Washington, DC; and Charleston. A black unit of the US Cavalry was even attacked by a white mob in Bisbee, Arizona.

On a warm spring day in downtown Tulsa, a young white girl, Sarah Page, stood waiting at her post at the controls of an elevator on the first floor of the Drexel Building on Main Street. It was 1921, and manual elevator operators like Sarah used a control lever to drive the cars up and down at the command of passengers. It was a routine job, but she was 17 years old and just starting out.

In a quiet hour of that afternoon, she saw Dick Rowland, who was black. He was a young shoe shiner who worked in the same building. Rowland approached the elevator and stepped inside. Then something happened.

The Tulsa newspapers were never clear on exactly what it was. But a clerk who heard a commotion in the elevator brought it to the attention of the police. Rowland was arrested for assault and locked up in a jail cell at the top floor of the county courthouse. Some people demanded that Rowland be lynched for his alleged assault. His arrest brought crowds of armed white men to the Tulsa courthouse. They demanded the sheriff hand over his prisoner, but the sheriff refused. When a group of black men arrived to prevent a lynching, shots rang out. Chaos erupted in the city between black and white residents.

RACE RIOTS

Race riots did not end after the Tulsa disaster of 1921. Civil disturbances were common during the civil rights era of the 1960s, and one of the most destructive riots in US history took place in Los Angeles, California, in 1992. Racial tensions still rise after confrontations between African Americans and police officers. Although not all police shootings involve black suspects, these events— such as the death of Michael Brown in Ferguson, Missouri, in 2014—have set off several demonstrations marked by race confrontations.

Many homes were left devastated after the riot.

Over the next two days, white mobs raged through the Greenwood neighborhood and the rest of the city. They burned homes, looted businesses, and shot down black Tulsa residents in the streets. Firefights broke out along neighborhood boundaries. The governor called in the National Guard to restore order. Planes flew over the city, dropping explosives and shooting from the air.

By the time it was over, hundreds of people were dead, most of them black, and the Greenwood neighborhood was largely destroyed. Black families moved out, or tried to rebuild, while a mass grave was dug in a Tulsa cemetery. The city had experienced the worst riot in US history at that time. The event was largely overlooked in Tulsa newspapers and histories until the 1990s. That's when a Tulsa Riot Commission was formed to investigate the event. Also, the Greenwood Cultural Center was established to offer visitors photos, films, and texts related to the vanished neighborhood.

RACISM AND PROGRESS

The KKK, a relic of Reconstruction, was revived in the 1920s. The KKK aimed to keep the races in their traditional place, and it also took aim at Jewish and Catholic immigration. The KKK has thrived in times of cultural change and dislocation, such as the postwar 1920s, when African Americans were migrating from the South in large numbers and racial tensions arose in the Midwest and North. The KKK grew strong in Northern states such as Indiana that had no history of slavery.

Separation of the races, a key doctrine of the KKK in the 1920s and today, was then supported by the law— federal and state. Even as sharecropping, the last gasp of economic bondage, died out, racism persisted in the form of voting restrictions, school segregation, and Jim Crow laws that strove to keep blacks in an inferior position. In the present day, several dozen Klan groups still exist, mostly in the South and Northeast.

THE MODERN-DAY
RIGHT TO VOTE

The Fifteenth Amendment bars any state from denying a person the right to vote based on race. But many states in the South still managed to keep black citizens from voting. After Reconstruction, Mississippi led the way in this effort. In 1890, legislators wrote into the state's constitution a poll tax that had to be paid for two years before an election and that many poor blacks could not afford. There was also a literacy test. People who sought to register to vote had to read and explain to a clerk a section of the Mississippi Constitution. The clerks picked out the section applicants had to read. For black voters, clerks deliberately chose passages that were complicated and difficult to understand.

Although these methods of disenfranchisement are now illegal, some states still manage to suppress black voting. Several states require a photo ID for voter registration, knowing that African Americans who have low incomes are less likely to have one. North Carolina went a little further by barring same-day registration, early voting, out-of-precinct voting, and preregistration for 18- and 19-year-olds. All of these new restrictions targeted the voting ability of African Americans, who disproportionately use these features to cast their ballots. Radio commentator Michael Tomsic of North Carolina says, "More than half of all voters [in North Carolina] use early voting, and African-Americans do so at higher rates than whites. African-Americans also tend to overwhelmingly vote for Democrats."[1] These restrictions were struck down by a decision of a federal court in 2016 that found them discriminatory.

In the 2018 midterm election, there were reports of voter suppression tactics that targeted black voters in Georgia.

But African Americans also made important gains through the 1900s. Many served in the armed forces during World War II (1939–1945). Shortly after the war, segregation in the military ended by an order issued by President Harry Truman. In addition, in the decision in the 1954 case of *Brown v. Board of Education*, the Supreme Court ended legal segregation of schools. The Civil Rights Act of 1964 banned discrimination of any sort on the basis of race, color, religion, sex, or national origin.

SEGREGATION SUPPORTERS

Advances in civil rights did not come easily. During the 1950s and 1960s, when civil rights laws were being debated, many people held to traditional racist notions of segregation in schools and elsewhere. Political leaders, many but not all from the South, made a public show of opposing integration. What the states did to separate the races was the business of the states, this argument went, and not the federal government.

Governor George Wallace of Alabama declared the 1964 Civil Rights Act a betrayal of the Declaration of Independence and the nation's founding principles. "This bill is fraudulent in intent, design, and in execution. . . . It threatens our freedom of speech, of assembly, or association, and makes the exercise of these freedoms a federal crime under certain conditions," Wallace said.[2]

WHAT'S IN A NAME?

Senator Richard Russell of Georgia was a politician who steadfastly opposed integration of the races. Russell, who served in the Senate from 1933 to 1971, spoke out against proposed laws to ban lynching as well as poll taxes, which had to be paid when registering to vote and which were intended to discourage many African Americans from taking part in elections. Russell helped to write the "Declaration of Constitutional Principles," also known as the Southern Manifesto, in 1956. It declared the opposition of Southern lawmakers to the decision in *Brown v. Board of Education.*

The Southern Manifesto drew on the principles of states' rights, an argument going back to the writing of the Constitution. "We regard the decision of the Supreme Court . . . as a clear abuse of judicial power. It climaxes a trend in the Federal judiciary undertaking to legislate . . . and to encroach upon the reserved rights of the states and the people," it read.[3]

To honor Russell's long service, the Senate named its principal office building after him after his death in 1971. The issue of race continued to simmer through many issues debated by the Senate and the country. In 2018— which was 97 years after the Tulsa riot—it emerged once again, when members of the Senate proposed renaming the Russell Senate Office Building for the late Senator John McCain of Arizona.

Several senators, most from the South, spoke up. Richard Shelby of Alabama declared, "Richard Russell was from the South and, I'm sure, not perfect like George

Today's Political Divides

Beginning in the 1870s, in response to military occupation of the South and federal laws designed to improve the lot of formerly enslaved people, the South instituted sharecropping, laws that restricted interracial relationships, voting restrictions for African Americans, and segregation in schools, businesses, and public places. The struggle of Southerners against the Northern abolitionists and Reconstruction laws also gave rise to modern divisions in US politics. Modern political divisions often occur between the Republican (conservative) and Democratic (liberal) parties.

Liberals have supported the efforts of the federal government to enforce equal rights, equal opportunities, and an end to discriminatory practices. Conservatives have held to states' rights, opposition to federal laws on discrimination, and an end to affirmative action programs designed to actively promote the hiring of more black employees or the acceptance of more black students in colleges. Both sides have arguments to bolster their positions and attack opponents. Liberals accuse conservatives of racism and discrimination, while conservatives say that liberal policies are designed to keep African Americans loyal to the Democratic party.

Washington and everyone else in his day. But he was a well-respected senator."[4]

Perhaps the idea of changing the building's name was a bit premature, announced Senator David Perdue of Georgia. "This renaming thing because of one issue is somewhat troubling. The fact that it's been brought into this John McCain thing I think is inappropriate."[5] A debate in Congress and the media over segregation and Russell's legacy followed.

Even a century and a half after the end of the Civil War and of slavery, racial controversies emerge in matters large and small, local and national. Slavery helped make the United States a global economic power by allowing slaveholders and others complicit in the system to exploit the unpaid labor of African Americans. It also left a legacy of violence, discrimination, and division that endures in the 2000s.

DISCUSSION STARTERS

- Have you ever seen a situation where someone was being discriminated against? What did you think about the treatment the person received? Have you ever been the target of discrimination?

- Some politicians oppose federal laws against racial discrimination. Do you think such laws should be up to the states?

- The modern KKK still uses emblems, slogans, and passwords from the era when it was a secret society. Why do you think some members keep up old traditions such as wearing hoods or burning crosses?

1670
The colony of Charles Town is founded by English slaveholders on the coast of what is today South Carolina.

1726
Thriving Charleston exports millions of pounds of rice, which is a slave-harvested cash crop.

1776
British colonists in North America sign the Declaration of Independence, claiming a right to "Life, Liberty and the pursuit of Happiness."

1786
Georgia slaves plant, cultivate, and harvest the first cotton grown in the United States.

1787
Delegates to a Constitutional Convention in Philadelphia create the US Constitution, which decrees that Congress may not ban the slave trade until 1808.

1792
Construction of the White House, using in part the labor of rented slaves, begins in Washington, DC.

1808
A congressional law banning the importation of slaves goes into effect, but many states still permit the buying, selling, and transportation of slaves.

1837
The cotton boom in the South ends in a financial panic, with land values collapsing and many plantation owners going bankrupt.

1846
Cyrus McCormick moves to Chicago to manufacture the McCormick reaper, a device invented in Virginia with the help of one of his slaves, Jo Anderson.

1860–1861

Eleven Southern states secede from the United States over the issue of state versus federal authority in the matter of slavery. The Civil War begins.

1865

The Civil War ends with the defeat of the Confederacy by the Union.

1877

The Reconstruction era ends.

1921

A race riot results in several hundred deaths and the destruction of the Greenwood neighborhood in Tulsa.

1964

Congress passes the Civil Rights Act, which bans discrimination on the basis of race, color, religion, or national origin.

2002

A lawsuit is filed, seeking compensation for unpaid labor during the era of legal slavery.

2016

First Lady Michelle Obama reminds people that the White House was built by slaves.

2018

Some Senate members propose that the Russell Senate Office Building be renamed.

SIGNIFICANT EVENTS

- The Constitution, setting out the framework of the federal government, held slaves to each be worth three-fifths of a person in determining a state's representation in Congress.

- In 1808, a ban on the importation of slaves, passed by Congress, took effect.

- The Civil War took place between 1861 and 1865. Through the Thirteenth Amendment, passed after the war's end, slavery was banned throughout the nation.

- In 1964, the Civil Rights Act banned discrimination on the basis of race.

- Strife between racial groups continued into the 2000s.

KEY PLAYERS

- Frederick Douglass was a prominent author and US official in the 1800s. He was an African American and former slave.

- Cyrus McCormick and his slave Jo Anderson created the famous McCormick reaper.

- Abraham Lincoln led the Union during the Civil War and ended slavery.

- The Ku Klux Klan used violence and threats to intimidate African Americans and stop them from claiming their legal rights as US citizens.

IMPACT ON SOCIETY

Slave labor was a major factor in the economic growth of the British colonies and later the United States. The debate over slavery divided the country and led to the Civil War. It also left lasting marks on today's social and political landscape, such as the debate surrounding reparations and the fight for equality in the United States.

QUOTE

"I wake up every morning in a house that was built by slaves."

—*First Lady Michelle Obama, 2016*

abolition

The act of officially banning something.

cash crop

A crop grown for sale or export, such as coffee, tobacco, or cotton.

collateral

Property, at one time including slaves, pledged to a money lender to secure the repayment of a loan.

disenfranchisement

The state of having been deprived of a legal right, such as voting.

firefight

A conflict that involves gunfire.

Jim Crow laws

State and local laws passed in the 1880s in the South to racially segregate black people.

lynch

To kill someone illegally as punishment for a perceived crime.

plaintiff

The one accusing a defendant in a court of law.

plantation

A large farm or estate where crops such as cotton, sugar, and tobacco are grown, usually by laborers who live on the estate.

Reconstruction

The era after the Civil War when the Southern states rebuilt and reorganized.

reparation

Compensation required from a nation for damage or injury done to a person or group of people.

secession

The formal withdrawal of one group or region from a political union.

segregation

The practice of separating groups of people based on race, gender, ethnicity, or other factors.

sharecropping

The practice of farming another person's land and using the crop as rent payment.

SELECTED BIBLIOGRAPHY

Baptist, Edward E. *The Half Has Never Been Told: Slavery and the Making of American Capitalism*. Basic, 2016.

Furstenberg, François. *In the Name of the Father: Washington's Legacy, Slavery, and the Making of a Nation*. Penguin, 2006.

Schermerhorn, Calvin. *The Business of Slavery and the Rise of American Capitalism, 1815–1860*. Yale UP, 2015.

FURTHER READINGS

Bakshi, Kelly. *Roots of Racism*. Abdo, 2018.

Davis, Kenneth C. *In the Shadow of Liberty: The Hidden History of Slavery, Four Presidents, and Five Black Lives*. Henry Holt, 2016.

Hamen, Susan E. *Civil War Aftermath and Reconstruction*. Abdo, 2017.

ONLINE RESOURCES

Booklinks
NONFICTION NETWORK
FREE! ONLINE NONFICTION RESOURCES

To learn more about how slaves built America, please visit **abdobooklinks.com** or scan this QR code. These links are routinely monitored and updated to provide the most current information available.

MORE INFORMATION

For more information on this subject, contact or visit the following organizations:

AMERICAN CIVIL WAR MUSEUM
159 Horseshoe Rd.
Appomattox, VA 24522
434-352-5791
acwm.org
The American Civil War Museum provides visitors with information about the Civil War from both the Confederate and Union perspectives.

NATIONAL MUSEUM OF AFRICAN AMERICAN HISTORY & CULTURE
1400 Constitution Ave. NW
Washington, DC 20560
844-750-3012
nmaahc.si.edu
The National Museum of African American History & Culture opened in 2016. This museum has tens of thousands of artifacts illuminating African American history and culture, including exhibits on the history of slavery.

SOURCE NOTES

CHAPTER 1. WHAT SLAVERY BUILT

1. Kiran Krishnamurthy. "Sandstone in Washington Buildings Came from Island on Aquia Creek." *Baltimore Sun*, 30 Sept. 2002, articles.baltimoresun.com. Accessed 18 Dec. 2018.

2. Michael Daly. "What We Owe the White House Slaves: $83 Million." *Daily Beast*, 27 July 2016, thedailybeast.com. Accessed 18 Dec. 2018.

3. Daly, "What We Owe the White House Slaves."

4. Callum Borchers. "How the Media Covered Michelle Obama's 'House That Was Built by Slaves' Line." *Washington Post*, 26 July 2016, washingtonpost.com. Accessed 18 Dec. 2018.

5. "Jordan B. Noble." *National Park Service*, n.d., nps.gov. Accessed 18 Dec. 2018.

CHAPTER 2. CHARLESTON

1. "South Carolina and the African Slave Trade." *Sciway*, n.d., sciway.net. Accessed 18 Dec. 2018.

2. Brian Hicks. "Slavery in Charleston: A Chronicle of Human Bondage in the Holy City." *Post and Courier*, 9 Apr. 2011, postandcourier.com. Accessed 18 Dec. 2018.

3. Henry C. Dethloff. "The Colonial Rice Trade." *Agricultural History*, vol. 56, no. 1, 1982, p. 232, jstor.org. Accessed 18 Dec. 2018.

4. Abigail Darlington. "Why Charleston's Slavery Apology Barely Passed City Council." *Post and Courier*, 24 June 2018, postandcourier.com. Accessed 18 Dec. 2018.

5. Dethloff, "The Colonial Rice Trade," 237.

6. Dethloff, "The Colonial Rice Trade," 238.

7. "Charles Town." *National Humanities Center*, n.d., nationalhumanitiescenter.org. Accessed 18 Dec. 2018.

CHAPTER 3. COMPROMISES WITH SLAVERY

1. "George Washington's Last Will and Testament, 9 July 1799." *National Archives*, n.d., founders.archives.gov. Accessed 18 Dec. 2018.

2. "Tobacco Timeline." *Tobacco.org*, n.d., archive.tobacco.org. Accessed 10 Sept. 2018.

3. "Tobacco Timeline."

4. "Tobacco Timeline."

5. "Declaration of Independence: A Transcription." *National Archives*, n.d., archives.gov. Accessed 18 Dec. 2018.

6. "U.S. Constitution." *Cornell's Legal Information Institute*, n.d., law.cornell.edu. Accessed 18 Dec. 2018.

7. "George Mason's Views on Slavery." *Gunston Hall*, n.d., gunstonhall.org. Accessed 18 Dec. 2018.

8. Frederick Douglass. *The Life and Times of Frederick Douglass*. Citadel, 1983. 267.

CHAPTER 4. SLAVERY, TRADE, AND POLITICS

1. "The Particular Customs and Manners." *American Studies at the University of Virginia*, n.d., xroads.virginia.edu. Accessed 18 Dec. 2018.

2. "George Mason's Views on Slavery." *Gunston Hall*, n.d., gunstonhall.org. Accessed 18 Dec. 2018.

3. Sven Beckert and Seth Rockman (eds). *Slavery's Capitalism: A New History of American Economic Development*. U of P Press, 2016. 107.

4. George R. Lamplugh. "Yazoo Land Fraud." *New Georgia Encyclopedia*, 8 June 2017, georgiaencyclopedia.org. Accessed 18 Dec. 2018.

5. "Slavery and Justice." *Brown University*, n.d., brown.edu. Accessed 18 Dec. 2018.

CHAPTER 5. THE COTTON ECONOMY

1. Sven Beckert and Seth Rockman (eds). *Slavery's Capitalism: A New History of American Economic Development.* U of P Press, 2016. 125.

2. Joshua D. Rothman. "The Slave Bubble." *Slate*, 9 July 2015, slate.com. Accessed 18 Dec. 2018.

3. Gene Dattel. "When Cotton Was King." *New York Times*, 26 Mar. 2011, nytimes.com. Accessed 18 Dec. 2018.

4. Sven Beckert. *Empire of Cotton: A Global History.* Alfred A. Knopf, 2014. 115.

CHAPTER 6. MAKING A BREADBASKET

1. "Nat Turner." *History*, n.d., history.com. Accessed 18 Dec. 2018.

2. Bonnie V. Winston. "Jo Anderson." *Richmond Times-Dispatch*, 5 Feb. 2013, richmond.com. Accessed 18 Dec. 2018.

CHAPTER 7. THE CIVIL WAR AND ITS AFTERMATH

1. "14th Amendment." *Cornell's Legal Information Institute*, n.d., law.cornell.edu. Accessed 18 Dec. 2018.

2. Rajan Hanstad. "Repealing the 13th Amendment." *Medium*, 18 Feb. 2018, medium.com. Accessed 18 Dec. 2018.

3. "Reconstruction." *History*, n.d., history.com. Accessed 18 Dec. 2018.

4. "Milestones in the Fight against Modern Slavery." *Reuters*, 31 May 2016, reuters.com. Accessed 18 Dec. 2018.

5. Rex Springston. "Happy Slaves? The Peculiar Story of Three Virginia School Textbooks." *Richmond Times-Dispatch*, 14 Apr. 2018, richmond.com. Accessed 18 Dec. 2018.

6. Becky Little. "Why the Confederate Flag Made a 20th Century Comeback." *National Geographic*, 26 June 2015, news.nationalgeographic.com. Accessed 18 Dec. 2018.

CHAPTER 8. RECONSTRUCTION AND MODERN AMERICA

1. "Aetna Apologizes for Slave Insurance." *Los Angeles Times*, 11 Mar. 2000, articles.latimes.com. Accessed 18 Dec. 2018.

2. Alemayehu Bishaw and Craig Benson. "Eight of Ten Most Populous States Show at Least Three Years of Decline Since 2012." *US Census Bureau*, 13 Sept. 2018, census.gov. Accessed 18 Dec. 2018.

3. "15 Major Corporations You Never Knew Profited from Slavery." *Atlanta Black Star*, 26 Aug. 2013, atlantablackstar.com. Accessed 18 Dec. 2018.

4. Danny Vinik. "The Economics of Reparations: Why Congress Should Meet Ta-Nehisi Coates's Modest Demand." *New Republic*, 21 May 2014, newrepublic.com. Accessed 18 Dec. 2018.

5. Marianne Williamson. "Why We Need Both a National Apology and Reparations to Heal the Wounds of Racism." *Washington Post*, 4 Apr. 2018, washingtonpost.com. Accessed 18 Dec. 2018.

CHAPTER 9. ENDURING RACISM

1. Camila Domonoske. "Supreme Court Declines Republican Bid to Revive North Carolina Voter ID Law." *NPR*, 15 May 2017, npr.org. Accessed 18 Dec. 2018.

2. Christopher J. Bosso. *American Government: Conflict, Compromise, and Citizenship*. Westview, 2000.

3. "Southern Manifesto on Integration." *Supreme Court History*, n.d., thirteen.org. Accessed 18 Dec. 2018.

4. Catie Edmondson. "Replace Richard Russell's Name with McCain's? Senate Debates a Segregationist's Legacy." *New York Times*, 28 Aug. 2018, nytimes.com. Accessed 18 Dec. 2018.

5. Shon Gables. "Georgia Senator Pushes Back on Plan to Rename Russell Senate Building." *CBS*, 28 Aug. 2018, cbs46.com. Accessed 18 Dec. 2018.

DUCHESS HARRIS, JD, PHD

Dr. Harris is a professor of American Studies at Macalester College and curator of the Duchess Harris Collection of ABDO books. She is also the coauthor of the titles in the collection, which features popular selections such as *Hidden Human Computers: The Black Women of NASA* and series including News Literacy and Being Female in America.

Before working with ABDO, Dr. Harris authored several other books on the topics of race, culture, and American history. She served as an associate editor for *Litigation News*, the American Bar Association Section of Litigation's quarterly flagship publication, and was the first editor in chief of *Law Raza*, an interactive online journal covering race and the law, published at William Mitchell College of Law. She has earned a PhD in American Studies from the University of Minnesota and a JD from William Mitchell College of Law.

TOM STREISSGUTH

Tom Streissguth has authored more than 100 books on many different subjects, including geography, history, sports, and current events. He attended Yale University, where he majored in music, and he has worked as a teacher, editor, and journalist.